THE
BUSINESS
BATTLEFIELD

9 Warrior Principles to
protect, grow *and* **simplify**
your business

For information, address
Navigator Press, Inc.,
2700 Patriot Blvd. - Suite 440
Glenview, IL 60026

Book design: Jess Poisl

CONTENTS

» INTRODUCTION

Business is war. Well, at least it is a daily fight-it-out-in-the-trenches type of war. Business owners are stretched. They wear too many hats with too few resources and too little time to accomplish anything. That is the bad news.

The good news is it's a whole new world out there. Never in the history of mankind has the playing field been so level. Anyone can start a business easily with an Internet connection and a feasible, marketable idea.

The challenge for the established business: more competition with each new technology. In some cases, your business might need a complete overhaul. At a minimum, it will require a new phase of discipline that incorporates ongoing education, innovation and communication.

When we were preparing to write this book, the idea of war struck us as relevant to the business world. In this slow-growth, post-Great Recession environment, it seems akin to the unyielding desperate war in the trenches during the Great War of the early 20th century.

That got us thinking. If business is like war, just fought on a different ground with slightly different rules, what are the appropriate principles?

For those of you who are military history buffs, there are nine very well-established principles of warfare. They are:

- Mass
- Objective
- Offensive
- Surprise
- Economy of force
- Maneuver
- Unity of command
- Security
- Simplicity

History bears out that the great commanders who utilized the majority of these nine principles during their operations ultimately succeeded in winning the war.

In a similar way, we have compiled nine warrior principles of business to utilize in the daily battles we face in running successful businesses.

- Growth
- Confidence
- Goals
- Process
- Optimism
- Marketing
- Innovation
- Learning
- Clarity

One may be able to make some direct overlap with the principles of warfare, but not entirely.

This book is meant to be a quick read. Something you can

pick up and finish in an hour on any plane ride around the country. The intent is to provide you, the business owner, several good ideas you can implement in your business. If you run a growth-oriented business with an eager eye toward clarity of mind and focus of business purpose, then read on.

» FOCUS ON GROWTH

Without continual growth and progress, such words as improvement, achievement and success have no meaning.

-BENJAMIN FRANKLIN

Growth, in some curious way, I suspect, depends on being always in motion just a little bit, one way or another.

-NORMAN MAILER

The best way to predict the future is to invent it.

-ALAN KAY

A business enterprise is either growing or dying. There is no in-between. No status quo. When we see a business marking time, it will not be long before the plant is shuttered, the business closed, the inventory and equipment sold. Not a pretty sight. When it comes to the health of a business, there is only one option: growth.

Growing a business can be like looking up a steep slope into the sun with the wind in your face and no guide posts or signs saying "this way." It is like drinking from a fire hose, or trying to take a deep lungful of fresh air as you frantically labor to move forward.

The world does not stop. We somehow have to keep one foot in the present operating, cash-flowing company, the other in the future envisioned enterprise. Fortunately, there is an approach to make moving forward a bit easier.

Imagine you are at the top of a future mountain of growth. Take it all in and clearly delineate what this vision of the future is. We're asking you to consider jumping forward in time. Build yourself a picture of the future.

Describe and write down all that you see. Write down what it looks like. Seriously—<u>Write</u> <u>It</u> <u>Down</u>. Your employees will thank you. We can only turn on the power of our creative mind when we define what it is we want to achieve. We can only build that future structure when people have an image of what it should look like.

Make sure they are concrete, tangible, measurable things. What new products or services have you created? How are your customers or clients reaping the benefits of your new growth and the new value you have created for them? When you look back toward the present, what obstacles did you have to overcome? What new capabilities did you develop and achieve?

Seeing and describing the future first makes it easier to climb your new mountain of growth. It is a technique to pull you and your company forward. You and your team will figure out the path ahead and guide your business forward from the present to that future vision.

There is another element about building your future

business that is critical — make the future seem normal. Make it feel as normal as your present company. First visualize; then create a new normal in your mind.

As normal as a box: We can all picture a box. It has structure; it's familiar. We all crave structure in our lives. The homes we live in, the roads we drive on, the hours we work, and the routines of daily living are well-defined and familiar. Without these structures, the world would be completely chaotic, confusing and random.

Similarly for a business, the physical walls, the processes, the products and the services all function around structure. Our employees recognize it; our clients recognize it. It's our current normal.

At some point in the past your current company was at the top of the previous mountain of growth. It was a dream that took years to build. In the process of building the company, the dream turned into reality. Rules, procedures and processes were established. The staff began to establish routines. Commerce was conducted. The belts and suspenders of operating the business were identified and established. You built your box.

To grow a new vision of the future, a new company of the future, a new and unfamiliar box, needs to be designed. The image of this new box needs to be completely defined. The outside, inside, underside and topside need to be inspected and internalized. It needs to feel normal. Once it becomes normal, folks have something concrete to wrap their arms around and work towards.

Communicating your new box is critical. Constantly educating and reinforcing what will happen must permeate the company at all levels at all times. Championing change to make the future company real is a concerted effort. It requires buy-in. All key leaders on your team need to communicate the message.

In the U.S. military, communication with a clear vision is the key. Officers and non-commissioned officers (sergeants) constantly communicate and reinforce the mission. From general on down to private, they all know the mission (new box) and the plan to achieve it.

It is one of the primary reasons we have been successful on the battlefield. Everyone knows the mission. Everyone can adjust and adapt as they see the need to innovate, lead and champion the mission and vision.

What size should the box be? How big is the future of your business enterprise? Should it be two times the present company, three or four, or 10 times? Merely doubling output or profits or product lines doesn't get us nearly as excited as growing the company by 10 times.

You read that right. Enhanced 10 times growth.

See it, feel it, touch it, and be it!

This 10x growth idea was introduced to us by The Strategic Coach®*. The Strategic Coach®* Program, founded some three decades ago by Dan Sullivan, has coached more than 10,000 business owners and entrepreneurs.

Most recently, The Strategic Coach® launched their You x 10®* program. This program is designed for growth-oriented entrepreneurs and business owners who want to grow their companies. Not two times or five times, but 10x!

An audacious goal! But just consider companies you know such as Apple, Google, Amazon or Microsoft. All of these companies have achieved 10x growth multiple times in their corporate lives.

In a recent interview with Success Magazine, Dan explained that almost all of the business owners and entrepreneurs in his coaching program have already grown by 10x during their business careers. Many have done this two or three times.

You may be saying to yourself: But I'm not an Amazon, or an Apple, or a Google. I'm just a print supplier, a manufacturer, a software developer. How can I compare my company to these giants and their growth by 10 times?

First, consider the statement by one of the most influential scientists of the 20th century, Albert Einstein. He said: "Problems cannot be solved by the same level of thinking that created them." Find new solutions for growth and any other facet of your business that requires change in order to achieve growth.

To change thinking and continue on your growth path, you need some attitude, moxie and good tools. We have provided a few tools below; some of these you may do already. *Designate a "canary in the coal mine."* Identify and deputize someone in your organization who is immune to your way of doing business and can point out when you are becoming the status quo.

You've heard of these situations. There is no longer focus on your customer's needs; all eyes are only looking to the organizational needs. Those times when innovation and creativity take a backseat to ordered change, incremental improvement, and protecting the brand as a core philosophy and belief.

Your canary guards against being engulfed in your own system and thinking.

Kurt Godel, the famous Austrian-American logician, mathematician and philosopher stated: "To understand the system you are in, you have to get outside of it."

Embrace life-long learning. Knowledge is a double-edged sword. Companies can be too knowledgeable of their own industry and start to "become the industry."

That is the reason why, time after time, small start-up businesses or businesses from other industries creatively destroy large status quo behemoth businesses: Ford over the horse and carriage; Jobs and the recording industry; Wikipedia and the encyclopedia and publishing businesses; Cable TV over the networks. It's the long list of dinosaurs trapped in their own weighty, safe, secure businesses.

Life-long learning needs to become a core philosophy and competency of the owner and hopefully of key staff in any business. Gone are the days of attending undergraduate and graduate courses and then expecting that knowledge to serve you through 40 years of a healthy enterprise. There is too much change taking place not to be exposed to new ways of thinking, operating and evolving.

Knowledge is fleeting. Learn to know what you don't know. Expose yourself and your key staff to everything going on in the world around you. Lifelong learning is no longer an option; it is a must, especially if you're going to grow your business.

Reject Negativity. The expansion of mass media in our lives, the dissemination of information through the Internet, social media, television, and yes, still word of mouth, has accelerated at an astounding rate over the past two decades. It is both a great advantage and great equalizer. It flattens (Thomas Friedman, *The World Is Flat*) the playing field.

But there is the dark side as well: negativity.

Did you know that of the 600-plus words for emotion in the English language, more than 65% are for negative emotions? Fear, hate, sorrow, despair…need we go on? These negative emotions permeate through the news media, Internet and advertising and perniciously wiggle their way into our lives. The antidote is not easy. We need a daily dose of something to combat the millions of forms of negative flu messages.

Consider this one daily routine: Every time a meeting of two or more people takes place in your company, consider opening and closing every meeting the same way. At the beginning of each meeting, each person answers the question, "What are you excited about right now?" You will be amazed at how it effects the energy in the room. And at the end of the meeting ask, "What did you get out of the meeting today?"

These two simple questions will inoculate you and your team against the pressing wall of daily negativity. The Strategic Coach®* Program teaches a form of this technique to its business owners and entrepreneurs. It is an effective way to maintain a positive outlook in a seemingly negative world.

There are many other ways to make certain you stay on a growth path, which limited time and space do not allow here. Forward momentum, no matter how big or small, is growth. Growth is the only path to continually operating a successful enterprise. Growth promotes an environment of excitement, new capability and transformation. It is what moves others to act, to be excited about the future, and to wholeheartedly get behind any enterprise.

The tools we have presented in this chapter, intertwined with those we will describe throughout this book, will support you as you take on the next mountain of growth.

»

- **Envision Your Mountain of Growth**
  - » Write it down
  - » Make it concrete and measurable
- **Make the Future Seem Normal**
  - » Completely define your new box
  - » Communicate, educate and reinforce what the new box will look like
- **Think 10X**
  - » Find your canary
  - » Embrace life-long learning
  - » Reject negativity ….
- **…. and Protect Your Confidence (read on)**

» PROTECT YOUR CONFIDENCE

A true leader has the confidence to stand alone, the courage to make tough decisions, and the compassion to listen to the needs of others. He does not set out to be a leader, but becomes one by the equality of his actions and the integrity of his intent.

-Douglas MacArthur

Confidence is going after Moby Dick in a rowboat and taking the tartar sauce with you.

-Zig Ziglar

One of the biggest killers of businesses is a state of low confidence. There is no greater reason why businesses fail than lack of confidence by its leadership.

Strong words, but true. We succeed mainly because we believe we can succeed. We forget this at times during the daily struggle to run our businesses. Confidence really is about your frame of mind.

A great example of this is Michael Phelps, who won 22 medals over three Olympics, 18 being gold. He creates this frame of mind through his routine.

Before every race it is exactly the same. He eats the same breakfast, goes through the same warm up, listens to the same music, right up to the time he takes off his warm-ups and ascends the starting platform. This consistent routine places him at a high level of confidence when the gun goes off.

During the 200 meter butterfly, his fourth event, at the 2008 Beijing Olympics, Michael's goggles started filling up with water with 100 meters to go. Despite this possible race-crippling situation, he went on to win his fourth gold medal of the Games with a seven-tenths of a second win over Laszlo Cseh. When asked later how he was able to win, Michael explained that his coach had him train in the pool in complete darkness so that he could maintain his composure and confidence under unexpected circumstances.

Confidence is not only a state of mind; it is also about a state of preparedness. For successful business owners, this is a daily fact of life. No business has truly proven itself unless at some point in time unexpected circumstances (bad luck, negative karma or whatever you call it) occurred, and then were addressed and overcome. The confidence, the grit and the determination had to be there for a positive result.

Protecting your confidence is also about the long-term maintenance of your confidence. "Never was so much owed by so many to so few": Churchill's words from a speech about the Royal Air Force and their single-handed efforts to keep the Germans from invading Britain in 1940. These young men confidently flew courageous missions that certainly shortened the war.

Over the last 30 years, we have had many crises that derailed confidence: Hyper inflation in the early '80s. The stock market crash in 1987, followed by the Savings and Loan crisis and recession of 1990/1991. The tech boom and bust of 2000, and the recent financial crisis and recession of 2008-2009.

It is interesting that during roughly the same time we also watched the rise of Steve Jobs with Apple and the Macintosh computer (1976 through 1984), unwisely followed by Steve's firing. Steve then rose from the ashes to first make Pixar successful, and eventually launched a successful return to Apple in 1997. The company's meteoric rise from near bankruptcy to become the world's largest capitalized public corporation is well documented.

Steve Jobs was said to be a difficult person to work for and was not dissimilar to singing artist John Lennon, who once remarked, "If being an egomaniac means I believe in what I do and in my art or music, then in that respect you can call me that....I believe in what I do, and I'll say it." These two artists had a lot in common. Both controversial; both extremely confident.

Jobs even created what many referred to as his "reality distortion field": His belief that the rules that applied to others did not apply to him. Where other public enterprises do surveys and exhaustive focus groups, Jobs performed a focus group of one—Steve. That is how high his confidence level was at most times.

What tools can be used to help protect your confidence?

Let's start with some basic blocking and tackling to boost and maintain confidence.

Accomplish just three things each day. More specifically, each and every day write down three things to accomplish. This sounds basic. However, you would be surprised how often we hear business owners say they feel like they "accomplished nothing today." If this feeling continues for more than a few days, watch out. We have the beginnings of a state of lower confidence and the results to follow.

Accomplishing just three things, any three things, keeps us in a positive state of mind with a corresponding high level of confidence. Just like asking, "What are you excited about right now?" inoculates you from negativity, completing three written tasks each day will provide a daily dose of confidence.

If this does not work for you, try completing a daily Positive Focus®*. The Strategic Coach®*, the entrepreneurial coaching program, has a straightforward form that can be completed in less than 15 minutes. In this Positive Focus exercise, you write down five positive things that happened during the day. Then write why they were positive, followed up by how to make them more positive in the future. Simple and powerful.

Some days you may be in such a bad place that the five things may be getting out of bed, eating breakfast, going to work, coming home and eating dinner. Pretty basic but it may be the place you have to start to gain back your confidence.

Business is tough. It sometimes feels like a constant

shelling—from competitors or customers or employees. The hits can keep on coming and may seem endless, brutal and unfair. However, you are the owner. You set the tone. You lead the company to success or failure.

The next confidence maintainer is the 80/20 rule. I'm not referring to Pareto's rule that 80% of the effects come from 20% of the causes. I'm referring to procrastination.

We have this sometimes false sense of "when" we will be ready to take on a new project, initiative or sometimes just the next action. There is this concern that all preparation must be completed before anything can start. Depending on the scale of a project, this delay can add up to days, weeks or even years. Or never.

The interesting thing is that no matter when you start anything, you only accomplish 80% of it right the first time through. The second time through, another 80%, then again for the third time and so on.

Why is this important? Because, if too many initiatives are in the procrastination phase, your confidence will erode. There are too many things hanging in the air. It is unsettling and creates clutter in your mind.

In the worst cases, absolutely nothing gets accomplished. You're pushing paper around, meeting to death, preparing to be prepared to begin to prepare for the final preparation. Insanity ensues. Businesses fail.

Procrastination is a confidence killer! Stick with the 80%!

One cure for procrastination that we like is the Four Ds. They stand for Do it, Delay it, Delegate it or Delete it. This is a rather simple exercise. It is like performing triage on your business if you find yourself in this constipated, confidence-killing situation.

This step-by-step approach has one very important rule. You may not work on anything without ending in one of these four actions. Notice the word action.

$\underline{D}$o it – complete the action right now.

$\underline{D}$elay it – file and schedule for a later date.

$\underline{D}$elegate it – immediately assign the action to someone else to accomplish.

$\underline{D}$estroy it (our favorite!) – place it in the circular file; the trash.

EXHIBIT A

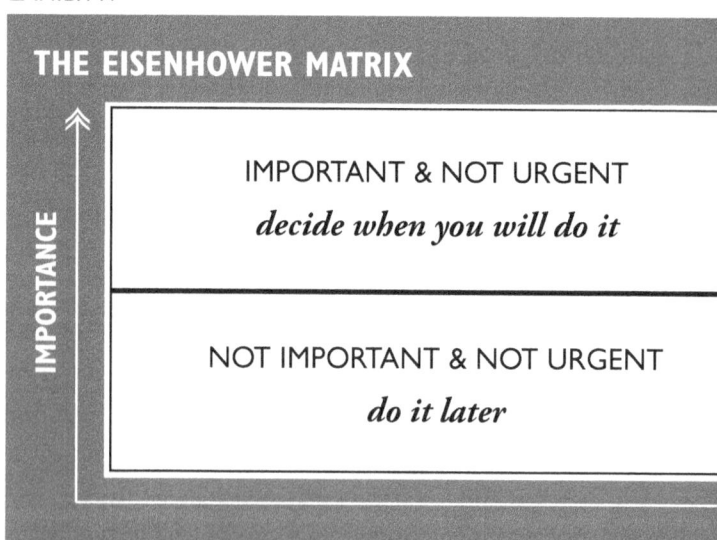

THE EISENHOWER MATRIX

IMPORTANCE

IMPORTANT & NOT URGENT
decide when you will do it

NOT IMPORTANT & NOT URGENT
do it later

If this approach seems a little too simplified for your business, then consider another version—the Eisenhower Matrix. President Eisenhower reportedly said, "The most urgent decisions are rarely the most important ones." Eisenhower's "4D" matrix (Exhibit A) is about learning to distinguish between what is important and what is urgent.

Most business owners live in a world of too many things to do and not enough time to do all of them. These Four D approaches help focus and direct you to the truly important items—those that need to be handled *now*, and those which may be juggled until later, when and if they become urgent and necessary.

Finally, we would be remiss without addressing the constant and increasing pace of change and its daily onslaught on every business. In the 21st century, businesses that survive

URGENT & IMPORTANT
do it immediately

URGENT & NOT IMPORTANT
delegate it to somebody else

URGENCY

and thrive have learned to change behaviorally when addressing the relentless creative destruction brought on by the microchip.

In Chip and Dan Heath's recent book, *Switch, How to Change Things when Change is Hard*, Chip and Dan examine this most important of confidence killers — change and specifically, behavioral change. Their entertaining, instructional book looks analogously at the most important elements of change: the Elephant, the Rider and the Environment.

The Elephant is your heart, your motivation. That thing that fuels your ability to move mountains. The Rider is your intellect, your reasoning and the one that directs the Elephant. Finally, the Environment is the jungle you need to navigate.

There seems to be an impenetrable jungle of people, equipment, systems, products and services. No one wants to take the time to change. It is just too hard. Too long and fraught with difficulty, disappointments and disaster.

To expect a positive result, all three elements must be in place. If your heart (Elephant) is not in it, there is no level of intellect or will power that will make it happen. Without direction (Rider), your Elephant will run amok all over the business, creating chaos and wreaking havoc.

Finally, and most important, without a clear path through the jungle (Environment), you will wallow in the mud and get stuck in the muck, feeling frustrated, powerless and confused.

According to Dan and Chip, while tackling behavioral change in our businesses, we all must Direct the Rider, Motivate the Elephant, and Shape the Path to expect a successful outcome. It is a powerful formula for success and a great confidence booster.

Eleanor Roosevelt wrote in *You Learn by Living: 11 Keys for a More Fulfilling Life*: "You gain strength, courage and confidence by every experience in which you really stop to look fear in the face. You're able to say to yourself 'I have lived through this horror. I can take the next thing that comes along.' You must do the thing you think you cannot do."

Never allow your confidence to wane. Keep the confidence-killers away. Maintain a consistent high level of confidence and there's a good chance you will continue to be successful in your business.

Always, always….Protect Your Confidence.

- Not just a state of mind, confidence is a state of preparedness and daily practice.

- Embrace Daily Positive Focus

  » Accomplish Just Three Things Each Day

  » Write down five positive things from the day

- Fight Procrastination with:

  » The 80/20 Rule

  » The 4Ds or the Eisenhower Matrix

- Steer your Elephant through the Jungle

» ESTABLISH GOALS

If you have built castles in the air, your work need not be lost; that is where they should be. Now put the foundations under them.

-HENRY DAVID THOREAU

If you don't know where you are going, you'll end up someplace else.

-YOGI BERRA

No good decision was ever made in a swivel chair.

-GEN. GEORGE S. PATTON

While this vision of the future motivates us to tackle one obstacle after another, how are we staying on track? Which opportunities do we grasp? Which obstacles do we conquer? How do we stay on course, direct the Elephant of confident, enthusiastic growth down the right path?

Goals — not vision or thoughts — but hard and fast written goals.

The key benefit of establishing goals is motivation. *In Drive, The Surprising Truth About What Motivates Us*, Daniel Pink discusses Mihaly Csikszentmihalyi, a University of Chicago professor and psychologist who, in the early 1970s, studied the positive, innovative, creative approach to life.

According to Csikszentmihalyi, people enjoy and are motivated by "autotelic experiences." *Autotelic* is from the Greek *auto* (self) and *telos* (goal or purpose). In his experiments, the goal is self-fulfilling and the activity is its own reward.

Csikszentmihalyi coined the term Flow. It's like play. We are in Flow when we naturally enjoy the process. Having fun on the job can be a gateway to real experiences and great breakthroughs. Like a smooth golf swing, a business owner at play (work) makes business look effortless. Put another way, it's like watching the soul of an artist expressing itself through business.

Think of Zappos, Google, Yahoo and other companies. They have these purposely playful environments with loose rules about dress, work hours, routines, and the like. They are creating an environment where motivation may flourish.

And, let's be clear here, it may cost $8 to produce one Apple iPhone in China, but the bulk of the price of the phone is for the creative work accomplished in Silicon Valley and other U.S. locations. It's good for business.

During my early adult life, I was not a big believer in writing down goals. I didn't need that. I wrongly assumed written goals were just a regimented way to keep on track to a fixed schedule of activities. Very boring.

But that changed once I fully understood the raw power

behind written goals. Once you understand why this works, you understand what motivates us to achieve new breakthroughs.

For some time now, behavioral scientists and psychologists have studied our motivation in work and in play. They divide what we do on the job into "algorithmic" and "heuristic" type work.

Algorithmic work involves performing a task step-by-step to a final conclusion. This could be stacking goods on shelves in a grocery store, delivering pizza pies, or suturing a wound.

Heuristic activities are those where there is no defined solution. It requires experimentation, creativity and "out-of-the-box" thinking to come up with novel solutions. Heuristic work could be developing a new product, reorganizing staff functions and responsibilities, or writing up a new ad campaign to create something new or different.

Heuristic-type activity is becoming more and more prevalent in the workplace in the 21st century. Algorithmic activities are declining due to technology and outsourcing to places such as China, India, Mexico and other third world nations. At places such as Google, Apple and Microsoft, one finds primarily heuristic-functioning jobs.

Heuristic work benefits from writing down goals.

Scientists have discovered that the act of writing, the physical movement of pen to paper, is akin to writing on the brain. It is a more direct way of emphasizing to your brain what you want to focus on. Suffice it to say that the subconscious works on what we tell it to work on. This all happens without our conscious awareness.

One common example of this very powerful ability of our brain is recall. You're talking to your friend about the movie *Casablanca*, and you remark, "Who is the actor in that movie? Give me a second. It's not coming to me right now, but I'll remember it in a minute." A few minutes later, the name Humphrey Bogart pops into your conscious brain and you blurt out his name.

What just happened? You asked your subconscious to work on searching your memory for the lead actor. While you consciously moved on to something else, your subconscious furiously searched out the answer.

Writing your goals down has the same effect. Why wouldn't you consider writing down your goals? Take it from a former non-believer, it works very well.

With this greater shift to heuristic-type activity, goals have now taken on a whole different meaning. We need more than ever to tap into the power of our brain. We need to write down our goals to engage our whole mind.

Although there isn't a direct correlation between left side algorithmic activity and right side brain heuristic activity, successful businesses are learning how to become more "whole brain" aware. Solutions can't be taught in academic environments. Math and science skills and education only go so far. Emotional intelligence, common sense, innovation and creative thought engage in creating new ideas, products and services.

Let's review some goal-setting basics. We need a Big Goal to provide the excitement and energy to pursue the future of the business we love doing. We need to direct our subconscious toward this goal, a much bigger future. We need to create a lot of new innovations and solutions along the way.

Shortly after the Normandy Invasion, General George S. Patton and the 3rd Army were given the mission to push the Germans back through France to Germany and ultimately capture the prize, Berlin, and end the war. With great tenacity, surprise and sheer determination, Patton covered 600 miles, chasing the Germans through various European countries toward Berlin. Each and every moment he and his men had one Big Goal: Seize the Final Objective, Berlin, and end the war. They were unstoppable.

Similarly, President Kennedy's famous speech of sending a man to the moon, landing safely, and returning to the Earth became a national goal that was the main focus of some 100,000 scientists, technicians, astronauts and workers for the better part of the 1960s. There were scores of algorithmic and heuristic activities accomplished by legions of people at NASA and elsewhere.

How do you find your Big Goal?

First, ask yourself a powerful question about the future you seek. There is a particular question we like, created by The

Strategic Coach®*, called The Dan Sullivan Question®*. It goes like this:

> "If we were meeting here three years from today, and we were to look back over those three years to today, what has to have happened during that period, both personally and professionally, for you to feel happy with your progress?"

This future-based question can quickly lead you to what has to happen over the next three years and all the way to today. Try it. Ask yourself the question, write it down, and build that future picture.

Be very specific; make it measurable, attainable and realistic. State it positively and make it understandable and relevant.

Another tool that may help as well is (see Exhibit B) the John Whitmore Model. This model is a great guide for writing down goals. The Big Goal may be simply stated as: The ABC Company will grow profits by 500% over the next three years.

Have you found the right goal? Does it adhere to the KISS Principle (Keep it simple, stupid)? Does it meet the requirements of the Whitmore Model?

The Big Goal is the most difficult part of goal setting. Test out this goal. Transport yourself three years into the future and look back to the present. Does this goal seem plausible? Is it realistic? Can you get your arms around it and get excited about it? If not, you may not have written it down

EXHIBIT B

THE JOHN WHITMORE MODEL

S SPECIFIC

M MEASURABLE

A ATTAINABLE

R REALISTIC

T TIME PHASED

P POSITIVELY STATED

U UNDERSTOOD

R RELEVANT

E ETHICAL

C CHALLENGING

L LEGAL

E ENVIRONMENTALLY SOUND

A AGREED

R RECORDED

correctly. Sit on it for a day or two, then come back to it and check it out again.

Once your three-year goal is established, it is time to write the one-year performance goal. It could be: Grow profits by 50%. One year is close enough to determine what needs to be accomplished between now and then to march toward the three-year goal, but not too far away to map it out completely.

The baseline for written goals is quarterly. Business runs on quarters. Our reporting, financial and inventory systems take place on a quarterly basis. A quarterly goal — or more precisely goals by department — is written at the end of each quarter for the following quarter. Department goals are in direct support of the company goal. Just concern yourself with the company goal for now.

The quarterly goals are where specific sub-goals are recorded. They could be to install an inventory control system; design, write and implement a new product marketing program; hire a CFO; or lease additional space for a new distribution warehouse. There are some goals that need to be accomplished during this quarter to set up for the next quarter's successful execution of the one-year performance goal.

I suggest you take one day a quarter and write down three to five key steps the business needs to take to meet your one-year goal. Share these and the one-year goal with your staff, so they can write up their own goals that they will need to achieve during the quarter.

Finally, all the tasks, activities and functions that need to be addressed during the quarter should be broken down into 30-day increments and listed out for the first 30 days, the next 30 days, and the final 30 days. Each department and each individual plays a role in successfully moving the company forward toward one Big Goal.

For you, as the business owner, there may be no more than a dozen tasks to accomplish in a quarter. Usually this involves the delegation and review of many staff members and departments.

The key here is to write them down and then schedule them throughout the quarter. You, the business owner, do not have to do this. Someone else may schedule these activities to allow you to do what you are uniquely qualified to do.

Business owners wear many hats and do a variety of activities. You set the stage, write down the major goals, and allow your team to do the rest.

We only work on what we ask our brain to work on. So ask it. Your productivity will soar. You will feel, more often than not, you are making daily progress. The company will move forward and focus on doing those things necessary to achieve the primary goal. And it will build confidence — for you and your entire organization.

Our most important asset in any business is our human capital. We attempt to keep machinery functioning at full capacity 24/7. Why not our people for at least 40 full hours each week?

As we move further away from algorithmic, rote work and toward heuristic, meaningful, challenging and creative work, written goals become so much more important. Clear goals, written goals, tap into the power of our brain to achieve new horizons.

»

- **Establishing Goals Drives Motivation and Flow**
- **Goals are Clearer When Written Down**
    - » Heuristic work demands it
- **Ask yourself the Dan Sullivan Question®**
    - » Write Down Your Responses
    - » Must be Measurable, Attainable and Realistic
- **Use the John Whitmore Model**
- **Write Them All Down**
    - » One Year Goals
    - » Quarter Goals
    - » Broken into 30-day increments

» EMBRACE PROCESS

Discipline is the soul of an army. It makes small numbers formidable; procures success to the weak, and esteem to all."

-GEORGE WASHINGTON

It was W. Edwards Deming who said, "If you can't describe what you do as a process, then you don't know what you're doing."

Deming is best known for applying his 14-point management process to educate the Japanese and help rebuild their economy after World War II. He was so successful at teaching the Japanese, especially in the automobile industry, that we lost our world dominance in that quintessential American industry.

What is a process? Are processes not all the same in your industry? Not necessarily.

A process is not just a series of steps or procedures. It encompasses philosophy, mission, vision and culture. Each business is therefore unique, with its own unique processes. No two are alike.

We market, sell, manufacture, manage, service and consult in uniquely different ways. There is some edge, some theme, or some special way that makes the business successful.

As an example, there are thousands of car dealerships in the country. Not one markets, displays, sells, communicates or services like another. Each customer ultimately ends up with a vehicle. Each customer has a different experience.

Or consider the hamburger. The large franchises of McDonald's, Burger King and Wendy's deliver hamburgers each in their own way. Some of us crave a Big Mac; others a Whopper; others a Wendy's old-fashioned hamburger.

Then there are the specialty franchises of Five Guys originally on the East Coast, In-and-Out Burger on the West Coast, and Culver's in the Midwest. Finally, there are the one-off mom-and-pop burger stands. Not one burger is the same. Not one experience is the same. Not one process is the same.

The key is the process. Identify it and name it. Make it real and palpable.

So what's in a name? A name is everything for you. It takes on a character and a being. Just saying we sell cars or sell hamburgers doesn't give any context to the core business value proposition.

Burgers are named. The process behind preparing, cooking, dressing up, packaging and delivering each burger is unique. Cars are named. Along with their respective manufacturing, delivery and service processes.

We love putting names to things. We identify an experience and a feeling with a name. iPhone, Four Seasons and Disney World all evoke a certain memory around a unique experience. It's not necessarily the actual device, or the buildings. It's more than that. Experiences are much more powerful than things.

And the name encompasses all of that.

This may be the time when you say to yourself: "There is no easy way to name my process." I agree. This is not easy. It's far easier to just allow the institutional knowledge gained by your company to remain in the heads of each employee.

Keep in mind; it's not about the name. It's about what you create through your process—your customers' experience, your employees' experiences. If you can clearly describe what you do in the process, if you can name it, they will experience it and you will own it.

Keep it clear and simple. We recommend between three and five steps.

Think about how you deliver your product or service. You can probably boil it down to a three-to-five-step process.

You may have a 32-point checklist or 16-stage manufacturing process for a device or for delivering a service. Although each of those actions is critical to success, stick with three to five identifiable steps. People will be able to get their arms around it and connect more easily with it.

Here's an incredibly complex process broken down into just two steps. In January 1991, General Norman Schwarzkopf and his commanders put together a plan during the first Gulf War to take back Kuwait from the Iraqis. They used the Hammer and Anvil Strategy.

The name explains the process: Move an infantry force from the south (Anvil) out of Saudi Arabia while fast-moving cavalry (tanks) from the west (Hammer) push the Iraqis toward the infantry. There were hundreds of critical steps, but this clear two-step process provided the vision and purpose.

One week later, riveted to our television sets, we all watched General Schwarzkopf walk us through the complete success of this strategy.

A strategy leading to a simple step-by-step process works.

People gravitate toward clear processes. Good processes place structure in an otherwise complex and frustrating world. And as soon as structure goes up, any flaws become noticeable.

Naming processes and steps in the process have a way of exposing the possible pit falls. More flaws are noticed by frontline workers than the business owner. But they need the identification of the process to improve upon it.

Let's take a look at naming a process for delivering group medical insurance. Learning about group health insurance can be excruciating for some people. This example illustrates the power of naming a process in a few easy-to-follow steps.

It's Friday afternoon. You've spent the last few weeks interviewing insurance agents about replacing your current group health insurance plan. It has become prohibitively expensive and you're concerned how the Affordable Care Act passed by Congress in 2010 will affect your ability to deliver employee benefits.

The fifth and hopefully final insurance agent walks in for an appointment. The interview starts off much differently than expected. You are being asked all sorts of questions about your company, your employees, and your past expenses with health insurers — questions about the long-term plans for your company, the obstacles you currently face, philosophy and culture of the firm.

It is a good conversation. It's useful. These are great questions leading to a valuable conversation with thoughtful meaning.

But you wonder: What does this have to do with replacing your health insurance coverage? So finally you ask, "How does it work? Where do we go from here? How can you help us address our health insurance needs?"

The agent responds she has a four-step process called the Make you Happy Medical Process. The steps are:

1. The Happy Healthy Checkup

2. The Health Plan Evolution

3. The Healthy Game Plan

4. The Continual Happy Health Experience

The names are made up to illustrate it's really about a current assessment, recommendations, implementation and annually re-assessing the plan to provide a constant high level of service.

You ask a few questions about each step in the process. The agent goes a little deeper and provides the stages within each step. She is more organized, knowledgeable, and intensely focused on you and your company. She wants you to experience a great delivery of services at affordable prices. You are very impressed. This agent's presentation is totally different than the other four. It is clear and simple. You understand what will happen over the ensuing months if you decide to go forward with the plan and process.

This is what naming your process will do for you. It clarifies your offering. It makes the complex simple. It gets everybody in your company on the same page. Moving to the next level is not only possible, you can sense a world of difference.

You don't just cook burgers, sell cars or sell insurance. You create unique experiences that are transformative and real. Naming your process will help grow your business. It is the reason the Japanese established their place in the auto industry. Deming would have it no other way.

To grow your business and simplify your processes, name them, then clarify them and improve them. It is that simple.

»

- **Describing Your Process is Critical**

- **Process Encompasses Your Philosophy and Vision**

  » Not just steps and procedures

  » Your philosophy is unique, so your processes are also

- **Name Your Processes**

  » 3 to 5 steps

  » Creates clarity for your team

  » Creates clarity for clients and prospects

» ORIENTATION TOWARDS OPTIMISM

I am an optimist. It does not seem too much use being anything else.

-Winston Churchill

Pessimism leads to weakness, optimism to power.

-William James

Perpetual optimism is a force multiplier.

-Gen. Colin Powell

What do the movies *Mad Max*, *Armageddon*, the nightly news, the environment, economic recessions and a cancer diagnosis have in common? Fear.

Fear overwhelmingly drives much of human behavior. "If it bleeds, it leads." Like gawkers to a car accident on the highway, we just can't seem to tear ourselves away from what we fear.

Studies show that the overwhelming majority (up to 90%) of news stories, articles, shows and editorials are negatively based. Our media are focused on reporting doom-and-gloom and the panic du jour.

Constant bombardment of this negative information relegates our daily life to a pessimistic world view. Optimism takes a back seat.

In business, this spells Disaster.

Why is it we are attracted to fear — like bees to honey? It's partly because of a basic part of our human physiology. The small almond-shaped amygdala that sits on top of the brain stem is responsible for primal emotions such as fear, hate and rage. One of our basic primary responses is to survive.

Survival, at the instinctual level, is to fight or flee. Stepping into the street and suddenly facing a Mack truck, or seeing a stick shaped like a snake on the ground, immediately triggers fear, flight and ultimately survival. Our amygdala is always looking for something to fear.

Beyond the fear factor, we have biases working behind the scenes. As Daniel Kahneman, a Nobel Prize-winning economist, explains, confirmation bias and negativity bias, along with an anchoring tendency, are key cognitive traits that affect our behavior.

Confirmation bias is our inclination to search for information that confirms our preconceptions. Negativity bias states we are attracted to and give more weight to negative versus positive experiences. Anchoring is the tendency to rely heavily on one piece of information. Just one observation, one event can trigger a negative response.

You need optimism to win your battles in business. Without

optimism you can completely miss enormous opportunities. In *The Rational Optimist: How Prosperity Evolves*, author Matt Ridley speaks about a group of 18th century French economists known as the physiocrats.

They argued that manufacturing produced no gain in wealth. They believed any economy that switched from agrarian-based farming to manufacturing would decrease in wealth. Over two centuries later, another set of economists argued that services were a "distraction" to the important business of manufacturing.

As we know, both groups of economists were just plain wrong. According to Ridley, today 1% of workers are in agriculture, 25% in manufacturing, with the remaining 74% in services, from dry cleaning, restaurants, banking and travel to entertainment. The physiocrats would be hard pressed to run into many individual farmers in today's general population.

That is a fact. Ridley combats pessimism with facts. Cold, hard, measurable facts.

According to Ridley: "Taking a shorter perspective, in 2005, compared with 1955, the average human being on Planet Earth earned nearly three times as much money (corrected for inflation), ate one-third more calories of food, buried one-third as many of her children and could expect to live one-third longer. She was less likely to die as a result of war, murder, childbirth, accidents, tornadoes, flooding, famine, whooping cough, tuberculosis, malaria, diphtheria, typhus, typhoid, measles, smallpox, scurvy or polio."

"She was less likely, at any given age, to get cancer, heart disease or stroke. She was more likely to be literate and to have finished school. She was more likely to own a telephone, a flush toilet, a refrigerator, and a bicycle."

All this during a half-century when the world population has more than doubled. Far from being rationed by population pressure, the goods and services available to the people of the world have expanded. It is, by any standard, an astonishing human achievement."

Facts can be powerful negativity eliminators. They can reorient you to a brighter, more successful future. You will find there are no limits to the opportunities to create.

The late Julian Simon, an American professor of business administration and an economist, is best known for *The Ultimate Resource 2*. In it he argues for the endless positive impact of human ingenuity. Simon believed there is only one natural resource on the planet, human ingenuity, and that human ingenuity makes everything else valuable.

Ingenuity leads to an abundant future. In *Abundance: The Future Is Better Than You Think*, Peter H. Diamandis and Steven Kotler present some compelling arguments on this topic.

According to Diamandis, the forces of experimental technology, the small back-of-the-garage inventors, the new technology philanthropists and even the world's poor "rising billion" are better positioned to expand our future.

Peter established the X PRIZE as an incentive to urge entrepreneurs to experiment with new ways of solving some of the major "scarcity" type issues facing the world. One of the prizes was a $10 million award for the first privately funded group that could put a spacecraft carrying passengers into orbit around the Earth two separate times within two weeks. That prize was won in 2004 by one of the 26 groups that competed without government aid, spending a fraction of what you would expect. That's powerful.

Most of the major problems we have faced over the past several decades from food shortage, overpopulation, freshwater wars, property escalation and depletion of natural resources have since been disputed. Rationally optimistic entrepreneurs such as Guy Mendez, Ray Kurzweil and others are expanding our horizons about what is possible.

Being oriented toward optimism is not about permanently affixing rose-colored glasses. Rather, it is about stepping back and taking a 10,000-foot view of the history of the business enterprise and reviewing the facts. Since the dawn of the Industrial Revolution, man has constantly improved his lot in life at an ever increasing rate of change.

There are a few basic rules to optimism, but one overriding rule is that optimism needs a leader. Winston Churchill delivered a speech to the boys at Harrow School in October 1941. In his booming, confident voice he said:

> "Never give in. Never, never, never. In nothing great or small, large or petty, never give in except to convictions of honor and good sense. Never yield

to force; never yield to the apparently overwhelming might of the enemy."

Churchill rallied the Britons to believe they could defeat the Germans, even though they had an inferior military with fewer resources. He was a great beacon of light, a rational optimist, who epitomized what great leadership with the proper outlook can achieve for a country in desperate need of hope.

To us, Churchill's leadership screams one clear message: Optimism is a you-based decision. You decide from moment to moment which side of the ledger to play from. Our natural inclination might be negative, but our logical inclination must be optimistic. We don't need to tie one or both hands behind our back to run our businesses.

Where can you find your own optimism? The best place to look is the future. In the chapter on growth we said to focus on a future that is much bigger than the present. A future orientation is an orientation toward optimism grounded in reasonable, attainable and sustainable growth.

As you look to the future, look for obstacles, too. We love obstacles. Obstacles create great thinking and great thinking leads to new opportunities.

Sure, we know there will be failures along the way while growing the business. We should be truthful in addressing those failures as they occur. Otherwise, our natural tendency to fixate on the failure will overwhelm us, resulting in a pessimistic, negative frame of mind.

Don't fixate on the failure; fixate on the opportunities. Our mantra is: Fail quickly and fail often. The quicker the failures take place, the faster learning takes hold and successes are ultimately achieved.

Optimism is a frame of mind, a frame of reference and a realistic lens to view the future. It's an essential weapon in your battle for success.

- Humans have a natural inclination toward fear and negativity
  - » It's physiological
  - » Biases are working behind the scenes
- Facts can counter negativity
- Human ingenuity leads to an abundant future
- Optimism requires leadership
  - » It's a you-based decision
  - » It's future-based
- Seek out obstacles
  - » They lead to opportunities
  - » Fail quickly and fail often

» MARKETING

There is only one boss. The customer. And he can fire everybody in the company from the chairman on down, simply by spending his money somewhere else.

-SAM WALTON

Most businesses don't last very long without successful marketing. Great marketing can move a lot of shoddy products — at least at first. Poor marketing cannot move anything.

Marketing is an elusive, slippery, ever-changing part of any business. One can throw a lot of money at it and produce literally nothing or invest very little and reap huge rewards. We sometimes don't fully know why customers buy our product or service. Even when we think we know, we may be proven wrong.

Peter Drucker, the famous management consultant, emphasized that business has only two basic functions: marketing and innovation. As he explained it, "Marketing and innovation produce results; all the rest are costs."

Businesses start with some new innovation that they believe consumers want to buy. If their innovations truly have merit, customers appear and write checks.

Along with the new product or service, there must be a way to market it to buyers. Drucker's innovation and marketing go hand in hand. Many great products have languished on the shelf and many expensive marketing campaigns have produced virtually no results.

We think successful marketing, supporting a company's vision, is like the columns of the Greek Parthenon. After 24 centuries of wear-and-tear from weather, earthquakes and war, it still stands today as a testament to time. Although the top of the structure is gone, those Doric pillars, the Parthenon's greatest strength, stand firmly beside each other.

Think of your marketing initiatives as those columns, equally designed and structured. Many different marketing pillars are needed to support your business enterprise. Marketing success requires a multi-column approach. No one pillar should be given preferential treatment over another — at least initially.

It's not dissimilar to the battlefield approach of Genghis Khan, a brilliant tactician. Although some of his methods were brutal, he clearly understood how to stay on the offensive when encountering an enemy. Offense, as in marketing, is a proactive measure to move forward.

Genghis Khan's men were horse soldiers, expert with bow and arrow. They employed a variety of tactics to slowly, methodically pick off their enemy using probes, attacks, feints, retreats and other tactics. They employed the full range of "arrows in their quiver" to gain success on the battlefield.

Many books have been written with thousands of different marketing ideas. We found two that caught our attention: "bullets then cannonballs" and "whiskers and cheese."

Many years ago when we started in business, the first axiom we learned about marketing was testing, testing, and more testing. To be honest, we often don't know why people buy a specific product or service. There have been countless surveys, after-action reports, studies, white papers and a host of research about this subject area.

All we really know according to the brain scientists is that the majority of consumer purchases are made emotionally. Some studies point to as high as 95% of all decision-making.

This may be very disconcerting. We like to believe we are rational, intelligent, reasoning beings. We like to believe we make a purchase based on cold, hard, irrefutable facts. However, study after study reveals something completely different.

As an example, a group of psychologists wanted to understand why, in general, focus groups rarely prove to be good indicators of the value and salability of a new product. In one study, they assembled focus groups to determine whether buyers would prefer to buy a red or blue hat.

Discussion ensued within the focus group facilitated by the psychologists. After some time, a few people within the group convinced the others of the value of the red hat.

When asked which color hat they'd prefer, the consensus was red.

For participation in the focus group, the psychologists offered each participant a hat from one of two boxes. One had red hats, the other blue. Amazingly, the overwhelming majority of the participants selected the blue hat as they left the room!

The action was in direct contradiction to what the group had agreed upon during the focus group session. In this particular study, the psychologists concluded that people generally tend to be non-confrontational. As far as red and blue hats are concerned, we tend to go along with the group even though we might make a different choice on our own.

We frequently don't know why people select a product or service. But, we can go about ways of testing and finding a set of rules for our marketing initiatives.

How do you go about testing? It sounds expensive. It could be, unless you adhere to the "bullets then cannonballs" technique that Jim Collins and Morten T. Hansen put forth in their recent book, *Great By Choice*. Collins focuses on long-term successful companies he calls 10Xers. These are companies such as Amgen, Southwest Airlines, Intel, Microsoft and others that have had long-term, successful enterprises.

In their book, Collins and Hansen emphasize three core 10Xer behaviors: fanatic discipline, empirical creativity and productive paranoia. It is under the empirical creativity behavior that the "bullets then cannonballs" marketing approach appears.

The concept of "bullets then cannonballs" conjures up an analogy of gunpowder-to-money. A business enterprise has a certain amount of gunpowder capital, to employ on marketing. Firing off a huge marketing campaign with a huge cannonball, without prior testing, is risky and expensive. Any first-time marketing shot can and many times will miss the target completely. Resources are then diminished for a second round.

Instead of first firing cannonballs, fire much less expensive bullets. If you miss the target, you learn and re-calibrate. Collins believes that business owners should be creative, but validate their ideas with empirical evidence. How? By marketing a new product or service in a low-cost, low-risk, low-distraction manner.

In other words, don't bring out the big guns until you can "see the white of their eyes." With limited resources and time, plus the potential for distraction, it is paramount to test and re-test.

Once you've identified the target, it's then time to release the cannonball. As practiced by the military in a mortar attack, "fire for effect."

Let's be clear, you first must have a good product or service that the public will clamor to buy. Through your innovation, these offerings have been built and readied for sale. It is now "show time." You now need to prove to yourself the "dogs really like your dog food."

There's a second strategy to keep in mind in your marketing efforts: more cheese, less whiskers.

With the arrival of the Internet and its search capabilities, we want our buying decisions to derive from education, consideration and information. To deliver that, consider a "cheese not whiskers" approach.

Dean Jackson is an Internet marketing guru. He and his good friend and fellow Internet marketer, Joe Polish, have a Web site, ilovemarketing.com. They have produced more than 100 podcasts about proven Internet marketing strategies, techniques and tools. They include interviews with other marketing experts as well as their own insights about what is effective today in Internet marketing. One marketing metaphor that Jackson uses: "whiskers and cheese."

He tells it this way. As consumers, we often face "the cat" as we are bombarded with marketing that is seeking a share of our wallet. The cat and its "whiskers" refer to company-centric advertising, which is all about the company promoting their products to us.

We are the cute little mouse. Mice are used by scientists in study after study because they exhibit the same basic instincts as humans. Seek pleasure. Avoid pain. The mouse's goal is to get the cheese and avoid the cat.

Most consumers hide from the cat. They try to avoid the radio, TV, e-mail, snail mail, Internet and social marketing calls encouraging them to buy certain products and services. The whiskers are everywhere, making people feel like they are being hunted to release their cash to these sales-hungry businesses.

As consumers, we really like buying things. They fulfill our needs and wants. But we have become more averse over time to being sold.

That said, ads about the "cheese" interest us. They're all about us. They are peppered with words like "you" or "your," not "I," "we" or "our." Ads about "cheese" engage us to enter into a dialog, a conversation about the benefits of this product or that service. It is not heavy-handed. Sometimes there's a free offer to allow us to determine if this product or service is right for us.

Think back to the Make You Happy Medical Plan in the Embrace Process chapter. Think how different and appealing that program is. That is a "cheese" experience.

A cheese relationship is a conversation. When you are sharing information, you are in a much better position to present your customer with actionable items — actions that they will permit you to present. This leads to actions they will be more confident to take.

Some of you may offer them direct information; others will send them to useful places to gain more knowledge. Whatever it is, you are helping them make a more informed decision. And today that is what more consumers are looking for.

The point is: more cheese, less whiskers.

This is particularly important when marketing to the Millennials (born 1980-2000). They appear to be inoculated from any kind of whisker marketing.

Eighty million strong Millennials are a bigger group than the Baby Boomers. They are just starting to consume products and services in bulk.

Millennials abhor whiskers. They love cheese. So should you.

Marketing today, more than ever, is about a Parthenon approach: testing with "bullets" and concentrating on the "cheese." Marketing is 50% of the focus of any successful business enterprise.

Focus is different than function. Many of your staff may be engaged in activities that do not directly engage in marketing. However, everyone should be oriented and focused on how their role can enhance your overall marketing efforts. That is critical to every successful business.

- Marketing and innovation produces results; all the rest are costs

- Marketing initiatives support your company like columns of the Parthenon

- Bullets, then Cannonballs

  » Marketing cannonballs are expensive

  » Bullets identify the target

  » Then fire for effect

- Less Whiskers, More Cheese

  » The Internet drives the demand for cheese

  » Consumers run from whiskers

  » Millennials, in particular, love cheese and abhor whiskers

» ENVIRONMENT OF INNOVATION

Innovation is the ability to convert ideas into invoices.

-LEWIS DUNCAN

If you always do what you always did, you will always get what you always got.

-ALBERT EINSTEIN

If it's stupid but works, it isn't stupid.

-ANONYMOUS MILITARY SAYING

The second half of Drucker's equation for running a profitable business is Innovation.

As equal partners, marketing and innovation are critical to growing a business enterprise. The scary thing about innovation today, certainly in the technology sector, is that it happens at a much faster clip than ever before.

We see companies go out of business in as little as six months because they take their eye off the ball. Anyone with a laptop or even a tablet and Internet connection is in business. The barrier to entry has dramatically decreased.

You may be thinking to yourself: Isn't innovation for those

creative types? Couldn't you, the business owner, simply delegate out innovation?

The answer, of course, is no. Not just because you are the business leader, but because innovation is the job of everyone in your company. The critical role for every business owner is to set up a structured environment that will bring out the best in people, a place where they can create and truly flourish.

In the Japanese auto industry, the structured environment utilizes Kaizen. Kaizen is the philosophy and practice of continuous improvement in manufacturing, engineering, business management and other areas of business. It involves all employees, from the CEO down to the mail room clerk. No idea is too small. These little ideas add up and can power an industry.

Other environments center around big ideas. This is exactly what Paul O'Neill did in 1987 when he was named the new CEO of Alcoa. Before Paul put the structure in place, he did something startling. When he stepped on stage to wow the Wall Street crowd about how he was going to run Alcoa, he spoke about only one thing: worker safety. He spent 45 minutes talking about how concentrating on worker safety was going to substantially grow Alcoa's bottom line.

Not surprisingly, Wall Street was unimpressed. Neither were his key officers and managers. Even after several months on the job, they wondered when he was going to shift toward being what was expected of a leader of a large, publicly traded, multinational manufacturing firm.

He did not and then things started to change...for the better.

Paul first required his unit presidents to report all worker safety accidents directly to him within 24 hours. In this large bureaucratic organization, this was a difficult task to complete. Each factory and division had to dramatically improve their communication capabilities in order to meet this requirement.

They innovated and quickly accomplished a better communication system.

At a completely different level, the union was still not embracing productivity. Worker safety? How could they not embrace that? One key safety issue they identified was molten metal splashing on workers, injuring them. The next innovation was a brand new pouring system. Not only did this innovation improve worker safety, it resulted in less wasted material and greater productivity and profitability.

Rallying around a singular issue—worker safety—Alcoa quickly hit record profits. The stock price improved dramatically, making them the darlings of Wall Street.

In Charles Duhigg's book, *The Power of Habit*, Duhigg goes on to explain that O'Neill stuck to what is known as a Keystone Habit—a habit around which many other good habits are spawned, resulting in a very productive and efficient manufacturing enterprise at Alcoa.

Paul O'Neill focused on worker safety. His officers, managers, foremen and line workers did the same. All of them had to figure out new ways to achieve this goal. The result was an entire organization innovating around a core goal. This is how organic innovation takes place.

While Alcoa's innovation centered around a concept, other innovations centered around a product.

In the summer of 1941, just before America entered World War II, the Army asked for a prototype of a new reconnaissance vehicle. It wanted the vehicle to be ready within a very short period of time in case the U.S. had to go to war. In fact, the Army wanted the prototype ready for testing in 49 days. Only two manufacturing firms competed for the military contract.

A few months later the Jeep was invented. A great innovation on its own, the Jeep spurred on even greater innovation when the Greatest Generation started to modify its uses. It was used for cable laying, as a field ambulance, for saw milling, as a firefighting pumper and for many other purposes. It became so popular with the GIs that it launched the first civilian SUV in the United States.

Emphasizing an idea or a product is a good way to get everyone focused, but there's more to creating an environment of innovation. You need to orchestrate innovation.

In *Human Action*, Ludwig Von Mises proposes that three requirements must be present for individuals to take action. *First*, unease or dissatisfaction with the present state of affairs. *Second*, a vision of a better state. *Third*, a belief that they can reach a better state.

We would add a fourth: permission and encouragement. Enter decision rights. Decision rights are first and foremost about getting the job done. It is about giving individuals enough rope to be free to innovate, but not too much to hang themselves.

Decision rights may be thought of as property rights in a business—similar to owning a home or 401(k) assets. Owners create decision rights by establishing clearly defined rules, responsibilities and expectations.

These decision rights allow each person in the organization to allocate, conserve or consume the business's resources as they attempt to innovate and create value. They enable your teams and individuals to know what they are responsible for and what they are being held accountable for, just like the owners of the business.

An interesting thing occurs when staff is afforded decision rights. Very soon, employees begin to show signs of leadership and ownership. They embrace their work and begin to earn greater decision rights (more growth).

They become better self-starters, more creative in their daily functions, and more innovative. Their unique traits and superior skills start to work for them. They set an example to others to do likewise.

It works very well. But decision rights do require communication and guidance. In steps mentoring.

Mentoring is often a very misunderstood practice. Everyone

mentors just by the fact that they show up for work and produce something during the day. It's the classic "being present."

Some are more present than others. They tend to be the better mentors. Because it all starts from leading by example. You can't be an effective mentor if your house is not in order.

Effective mentoring requires its own structure. We found that the Hersey-Blanchard Model (Exhibit C) breaks down in terms we can get our arms around. The model shows the stages of how employees transition from instruction to being coached, then supported, and then delegated to. During these stages, you see increasing expertise and variations of commitment. For the mentor, these stages require shifts in leadership and support.

You can see how this meshes with decision rights. As expertise increases and a sense of "ownership" increases, greater decision rights can be given. The model is not static. As we progress through one job and are ready for the next level, the model repeats itself.

We have a saying in our business: Every person is training (mentoring) someone else to eventually replace themselves. We are all replaceable. The world goes on whether we are here or not.

People do eventually reach the length of "their" rope. That is okay. We never really know how someone may develop until we give them the chance to show us what they can do. More than ever in history, the development of human capital has become paramount to continued business success.

EXHIBIT C

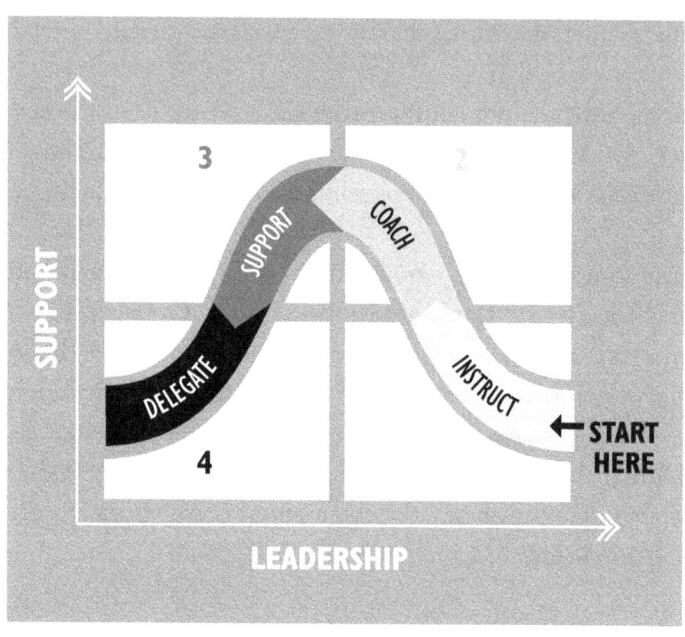

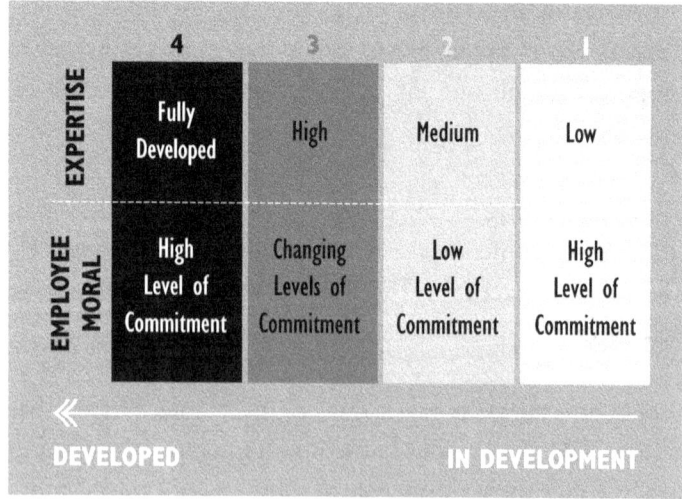

Read both charts from right to left.

People in the service sector, in particular, are largely underdeveloped. There's a huge potential within your managers and staff. Know that mentoring works.

This all comes full circle back to structure. Every business needs to have a clearly defined structure. As a good friend of mine always insisted at every single one of our business study groups, "we need a plan!" When I asked him why we need a plan, his response was always "because then we can change it."

That jarred my memory. This was something drummed into my brain in the military: Plan, rehearse, follow SOPs, "always do," "never do," and so forth. It seemed like a lot of regimentation. However, on the field of battle, this Keystone Habit of preparedness enabled the individual soldier to create and innovate. This is something the U.S. military is known for. They provide decision rights and mentoring through a chain of command to innovate. Adapt to the enemy. Try something different, adjust, and try again.

Business is like going to the battlefield every day. Things are changing constantly. Our people are our greatest resource. They can make the small adjustments (Kaizen); rally around our major objective (Keystone Habit); stretch to their limit (decision rights); and accept the critical after-action reports (mentoring) to fight another day.

It is that hard. It is also that simple. Successful businesses do those things that unsuccessful businesses fail to do. Innovation is not an option. It is an imperative. Everyone can innovate. They just need to be given the opportunity to do so.

You, the business owner, should strive to make yourself obsolete and unneeded. It is only then you know the business is running like a well-oiled machine.

»

- **You Are The Innovation Leader**
    - » Create a structured environment to bring out the best in people

- **Kaizen**
    - » Continuous improvement

- **Keystone Habit**
    - » One core Habit the business is focused on

- **Utilize Decision Rights**
    - » Clearly defined responsibilities and rules
    - » Employees take Leadership and Ownership
    - » More Creative and Innovative Staff

- **Incorporate Mentoring**
    - » Hersey-Blanchard model
    - » Instruct then coach
    - » Support then delegate

» CONTINUAL LEARNING

Anyone who stops learning is old, whether at twenty or eighty. Anyone who keeps learning stays young. The greatest thing in life is to keep your mind young.

-HENRY FORD

An organization's ability to learn, and translate that learning into action rapidly, is the ultimate competitive advantage.

-JACK WELCH

Veni, vidi, vici. I came, I saw, I conquered.

-JULIUS CAESAR

For many of us, leaving formal schooling was a relief from the world of academics. Entering the workplace was exciting, strange, at times a little frightening. The page turned, the book closed, no more education. True?

Yes and no. Formal education may be done. Real world education is continual. Unless you sought a professional career requiring advanced degrees. Real-world education has just begun. We just didn't realize the subtle shift.

At graduation from Basic Training in the movie Stripes,

leaderless Private John Winger (Bill Murray) responds to a question from General Barnike (Robert J. Wilke): "What kind of training, son?" Murray's reply: "Army Training, Sir!"

I can think of no better learning than the continual training our military goes though on a daily basis. Many new technologies first surfaced in our Armed Forces from continual education and applied training.

In business, lifelong learning is now critical. Not only to benefit yourself, but your entire team. You gain knowledge, pass it on to others, and watch it become instrumental to improving results in your business and keeping your company healthy and growing.

In the late 1980s and early '90s, we worked with three brothers who were running a 70-year-old manufacturing business started by their grandfather. It was a very healthy, profitable business with an established niche, supplying an item to the fast food industry. The product sold for pennies. They sold billions of them.

In the early '90s, while their business was chugging along with good profit margins, they turned their attention to investing in real estate in the Southwest. They concentrated all their efforts on this new venture and left a very capable general manager in charge of their plant and operations.

A problem surfaced when the annual contract renewal with their largest customer, who represented 30% of their business, came up. Their bid for the contract had fallen well short of two other competitors' bids. It took them a week to realize that a new technology had been developed that enabled the others to manufacture their mainstay product at a 10% lower production cost.

Their competitors had researched and invested the capital to purchase the machines. They had not and lost the contract.

When they tried to obtain the capital to purchase the new technology, their bank would not extend the credit because they had lost a critical client. Now, their enterprise was bleeding cash rapidly and about to lose the next two renewing contracts.

Within six months, they sold their business for ten cents on the dollar and shuttered the plant, leaving a 70-year-old business in ruins. What happened?

They failed to keep their eye on the ball. They stopped learning. Learning, seeking, researching what was going on in their own business. If they had been aware of the new technology, just 60 days before the first contract renewal, their bank would have loaned them the money and, in all likelihood, the contract would have been renewed.

Continual learning is not an option in business. Especially today.

Depending on the type of business, this learning may be more or less formal. Learning through on-the-job training. Learning from failures. Learning from rivals and from other industries. Learning by working **on** the business — not just in the business.

On-the-job learning has changed over the past generation. It used to be acceptable and practical to go through formal training to learn a variety of heuristic (right-brain) type jobs. There were formal sales programs, manufacturing training, management training and so forth.

Those programs still have their place, but have become less cost-effective and less time-efficient. Everything is moving much faster in business, requiring a more fluid approach to learning on the job.

The brain scientists come into play here again. Studies show that the more effective techniques for training new hires, especially in heuristic work, are through the fire-hose method. Inundate them with everything all at once. Think of it like infants thrown into a pool. Instinctively, they begin to kick their feet and thrash the water with their hands and arms to keep their heads above water.

We're not suggesting you drown a new hire with no skills. We assume they have some workplace expertise so that they have the rudiments of swimming in place. Now you throw them into the tidal surge to accelerate their learning! It's the fastest and most effective method of bringing them up to speed.

With all this fire-hose training, you will have to have a system to avoid chaos in your business. One system we wrote about in the last chapter involves mentoring. It can be a powerful tool to successfully get people learning and coming up to speed very quickly.

As important as good systems are, leadership—your leadership—is critical. Lifelong learning comes from the top. Leadership by example is always very important. If leadership is not embracing lifelong learning, then it's not going to take place anywhere else in your company.

In the service sector, especially professional services, knowledge is king. The more knowledgeable a doctor, lawyer, accountant, engineer or scientist is, the more valuable they are to an organization. Of course, only to a certain point.

In the last five years alone, the amount of new knowledge learned in the medical profession has more than doubled from the prior thousands of years of knowledge. That means doctors in their late thirties apply only half the knowledge they learned in medical school to their work today. No wonder each field of medicine is becoming more and more specialized, with ever-greater continuing medical education needs. There are over 18 sub-specialties (and counting) in the pediatric medical field alone!

The mantra today is to know what you don't know. Forget about trying to gain all of the knowledge necessary to understand everything in your field. If you spent 24/7 reading and studying everything that is new or being updated, you still would not make a dent in your knowledge gap.

Today, we need to steer clear of becoming *expert*, or at least believing we are an expert. It is a fleeting proposition. The fast-paced business world requires us to collect and review information in a conceptual format instead of in detail. This is something that is rarely taught in school. However, it is the primary course in "the school of hard knocks."

Knowing what you don't know allows you the humility to assume you may be wrong about what you think you know. This helps you avoid some pitfalls that could lead to the destruction of your business.

Let's make it simple. You really don't know anything. Well, maybe what's in front of you right now. Maybe the product or service you currently offer to the world. But there is someone out there right now who has created a better mousetrap. It's just a matter of time before you find out. Find out sooner rather than later. Keep your eye on the "I want to know what I don't know" ball. Building a network of fellow business owners—associates who keep up on the latest in their field and are connectors to many other people—is highly worth your time and effort. It allows you to learn what you don't know.

There is also a "curse of knowledge." Continuing to seek and learn strictly within your own industry removes you from the common man's reality. Each of us has our own acronyms, language, and way of communicating in our chosen fields.

 It can get so bad that we fail to communicate clearly to our customers. Our marketing materials, web site, product brochures and labels read like scientific journals, tech magazine articles, or medical device manuals.

The curse of knowledge shows up in everyday interactions. You make an appointment with the doctor to have a small rash on your arm examined. He takes a look and says, "You have pityriasis rosea." You ask, "Is it serious?" He starts reciting the possible causes and solutions using arcane medical terms that begin to frustrate you.

Before you know it, you're wondering if you have a serious, life-threatening illness. Then you ask, "Give it to me in plain English." The doctor says, "It's just a rash. Here's a prescription for some pills to take over the next week; it should disappear in a few weeks. Nothing to worry about."

Recognize your curse of knowledge and avoid it. You'll create a better experience for your customer and ultimately for your business.

Continual learning on the job, seeking out new technology, and knowing what you don't know—along with the dreaded curse of knowledge—are everyday issues that must be addressed.

But how?

One great way is to take at least one day each quarter or maybe even each month if you have the time, to work on the business. Schedule it and stick to it. Take a look at couple of formal programs, such as YPO (Young Presidents' Organization), Vistage (formerly TEK), Strategic Coach® and many other organizations. Many business owners belong to study groups, mastermind groups, or just informal gatherings after a game of golf to discuss business.

The structured programs all have the basic theme of a

once-a-month or once-a-quarter gathering where you get to work on your business rather than in your business. We think most people that are attracted to those programs come for two major reasons:

First, there's the content and experience of thinking about your business on a regular, ongoing basis. You get the opportunity to interact with your peers who are dealing with the exact same issues or perhaps issues that you hadn't even thought of. The industries may be different, but not the issues. You get ideas and work back and forth with each other. This is a great way to continually learn.

Second, it is a great way to re-energize, rejuvenate and reset yourself about your business. Your renewed energy will allow you to try out and learn from new ideas, to come back a quarter later to share experiences and improve on them.

If the group thing is not for you, try this: Take counsel from yourself. Schedule a meeting with yourself to review what is going on with your business.

Steve Jobs didn't belong to any formal groups. He was very successful taking counsel with himself and other key players in his field of view. Steve traveled to meet others, to share his views, or convince them to work on his latest idea.

He held countless informal hallway meetings where new ideas were discussed. He also meditated and struggled mightily with challenges at the same time sharing his most intimate thoughts with those closest to him. Steve had a continual learning program.

It doesn't really matter which way you learn. Use what works best for you. What does matter is that you embrace continual learning and that you do it outside of the realm of your day-to-day activities. Otherwise, you're not sharpening your axe; you're just keeping your nose to the grindstone. Technological change, obsolescence and other high impact events are happening regularly. You've got to be able to see them beforehand.

Sharpening the axe and adjusting the course has dramatically accelerated the pace of change. We're always amazed at how much we do during a quarter contrasted to just 10 years ago. We adjust more often, adopt new technologies almost every quarter, and our staff members struggle and innovate ways to keep up with the pace of change.

You may not know that adult education has become one of the fastest-growing industries in the past 10 years. No longer can one walk away with a diploma and never touch a book again. The school of hard knocks opens its doors every single day, 24/7, no holidays.

Business owners who keep themselves informed, seek outside knowledge, and flexibly meet challenges are, more often than not, rewarded with successful businesses.

Continual learning is no longer an option.

- **Continual Learning is Not an Option**
    - » Benefits all team members
    - » Its absence can be devastating

- **More Informal Training**
    - » Fire-hose method with mentoring

- **Lifelong Learning Requires Leadership**
- **Know What You Don't Know**
    - » Don't be an expert
    - » Build networks to knowledge connectors

- **Avoid the "Curse of Knowledge"**
    - » Leads to frustrated and confused customers

- **Schedule Knowledge Time**
    - » Work on your business, not just in it
    - » Take counsel from yourself

» GAIN AND MAINTAIN CLARITY

When people will not weed their own minds, they are apt to be overrun by nettles.

-HORACE WALPOLE

A lack of clarity could put the brakes on any journey to success.

-STEVE MARABOLI

Although our intellect always longs for clarity and certainty, our nature often finds uncertainty fascinating.

-KARL VON CLAUSEWITZ

Clarity is working when we're not thinking. When we act without thinking. Everything happens automatically. It is like making a great golf swing. It feels effortless, looks smooth and happens without conscious thought. Yet...the result is spectacular! The ball flies straight, and true, far down the fairway.

Operating a business can work the same way. This will be true if — and this is a big "if" — the fundamentals are firmly in place first and are clear to everybody.

In his book, *Small Giants,* Bo Burlingham refers to Jay Goltz, who started Artists' Frame Service in 1978 in Chicago. Like many struggling business owners, he spent many years developing and growing his business. Like many successful entrepreneurs, Jay worked hard at perfecting his business, which ultimately became the gold standard in the framing business.

Burlingham observed that Goltz has a knack for developing systems. These systems use clear and simple processes that he put in place. For the framing process, he has four basic rules everybody has to follow. They are clear and straightforward. The process is automatic and consistent. The result is seamless production of hundreds of finished framing jobs with 99.7% accuracy. The place runs like a well-oiled machine.

Throughout his company, Jay delivers clarity to his employees — both in terms of processes and expectations. He is a business owner who understands that putting all the elements together, with clarity on top, can make his business work smoothly and successfully.

How does this work in business? What do you see clearly when you're just trying to grow and run your business? How do you get your team to see clearly? We think it comes down to putting clarity on the top of a pyramid. Within the pyramid are your marketing, your innovation and your processes. Each of these elements requires a clear picture of your mission, your vision and your path to growth.

Clarity is Napoleon on a hilltop viewing the battlefield. It is Sun Tzu seeing 12 steps ahead towards a non-military, peaceful resolution to an ancient Chinese conflict. It is Patton visualizing his riding atop a tank through the streets of Berlin.

It's all the elements coming together that drive your confidence to move your business forward. While you face a constantly shifting and moving environment, it is clarity that helps you navigate through and execute seamlessly and automatically. With it in place, your business is fun, it's exciting, and it's successful.

Great clarity of mind happens when we ask ourselves great questions. Why? Because the problem is *not* the problem. The solution is *not* the solution. The solution is how to *think* about the problem.

In the process of thinking about great questions, key elements of our complex businesses float to the surface of our consciousness. Not everything at once—but enough of them to gain clarity about maintaining business direction and continuing business confidence.

In business, we want to be able to "see the forest *and* the trees." We want to engage our whole brain and see the whole forest with the right side of our brain, and the individual trees and elements of each tree with our brain's left side. Think of it as the 10,000 foot view, the tree-top view, and the close-up view of each tree. Business patterns emerge when we achieve this sort of whole-brain thinking and awareness.

In the past 10 years, brain scientists have unlocked many mysteries of the way we think, process information, communicate, and understand the world around us. Combining great questions about the business with a tool for displaying the answers to these questions is one of the best ways to gain clarity.

One tool that we use regularly is the mind map. A mind map is a graphic depiction of the answer to a focused great question. Mind mapping helps make connections between different elements. You can more easily recognize new patterns and interactions. A well-organized mind map provides a simple one-page representation of everything you desire to "see" about a complex situation.

It all begins with a great question. One of those questions we asked in an earlier chapter. Called the Dan Sullivan Question®*, it asks:

> "If we were meeting here three years from today, and we were to look back over those three years to today, what has to have happened during that period, both personally and professionally, for you to feel happy with your progress?"

We posed this question to a business owner a few years ago. He was looking to gain greater clarity about his already successful business consulting firm. Below are several steps that took place:

First, we wrote down on a flip chart all of the answers to this question and follow-up questions. We then began to build the mind map.

In the center we placed what his business does for his

customers. We believe that the best perspective happens when viewing it from what your customers receive from you—not about you or your operations. It's a subtle but very important differentiator. Without focusing on your customer, this exercise becomes just another back-office exercise in futility.

This mind map exercise zeroed in on the company's value proposition to its customers, to help identify its future path.

In Exhibit D are the results of the mind map that we created from the initial question. Notice how everything that is important about the business and its customers is on one page. Notice how the elements are factual, informational and conceptual.

You can see that there is complexity in the business and at the same time recognize a simplicity to it. That is clarity.

This businessman went on to refine his mind map until it felt right and was clearer each time he viewed it. He then made sure it was clear to employees and customers—a great approach to validating his conclusions.

It will help you get clear about things: you can cut through all of the noise and make some very clear decisions. Decisions about how to employ your people, your processes, your equipment, your products, everything involved when working with your business.

Now, it is time to build the stable bedrock of the pyramid of clarity. We need to explore a few other tools.

Recently, when reading *Great By Choice*, the latest book by Jim Collins and Morten T. Hansen, we noted that the authors put forth a very simple recipe of success: SMaC. SMaC stands for Specific, Methodical and Consistent. It is a formula for turning strategies and philosophy of a business into a simple list of do's and don'ts.

It has to be clear and concrete so the entire company understands what the rules are to work, live and succeed by. Equally important is that the practices have to be enduring. Regular changes to the rules can shatter clarity. The "C" — consistency — is critical to maintaining clarity.

No matter how well we strive to gain and maintain clarity, it may elude us. It does so for many reasons. One is entropy — the continual, ongoing breakdown of everything from a state of order to one of disorder. In the process of running your business, there is continual new learning and new growth, which tends to move your business toward complexity. This could lead to frustration and a feeling of powerlessness.

You will probably experience these feelings from time to time as you try to maintain balance between the other principles in this book. Many of the exercises we have incorporated in different chapters are exercises in maintaining your clarity. Setting a day aside each quarter to formally work on the business. Continually learning through formal and informal means, writing down goals and naming processes.

As each journey up a new challenging mountain is completed, clarity wanes. We must stay forever open to change,

EXHIBIT D

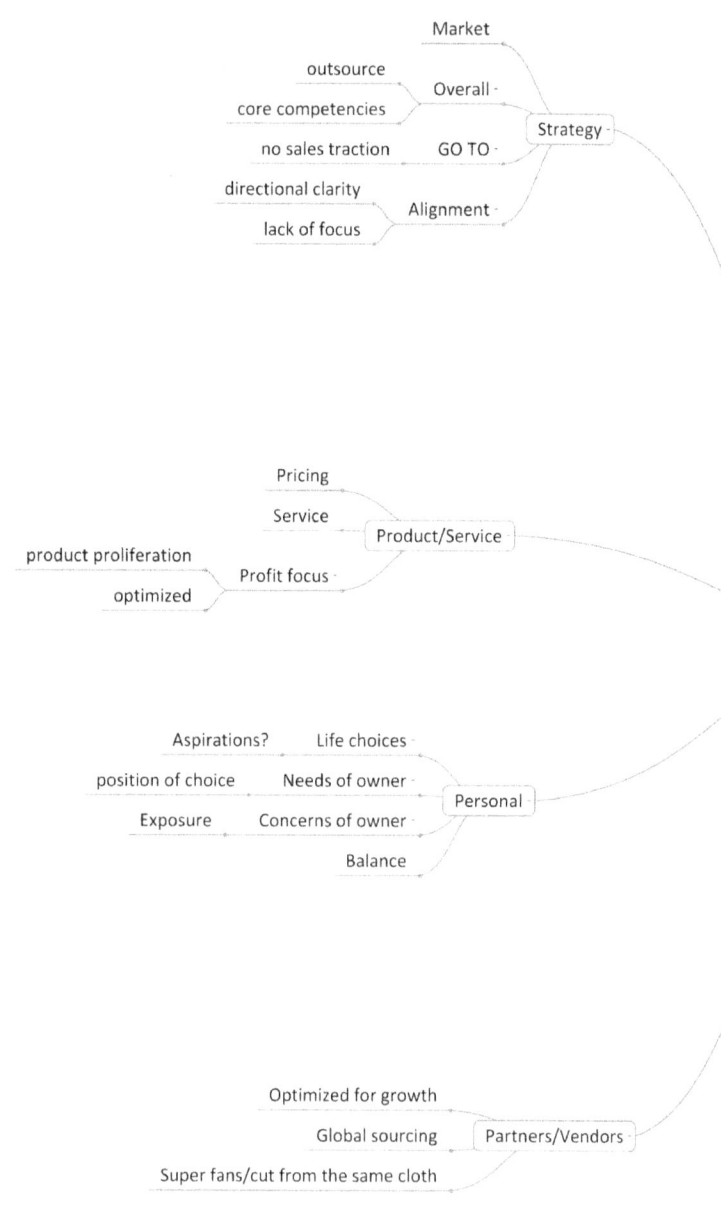

Market
outsource
Overall
core competencies
no sales traction — GO TO
Strategy
directional clarity
Alignment
lack of focus

Pricing
Service
Product/Service
product proliferation
optimized — Profit focus

Aspirations? — Life choices
position of choice — Needs of owner
Exposure — Concerns of owner — Personal
Balance

Optimized for growth
Global sourcing — Partners/Vendors
Super fans/cut from the same cloth

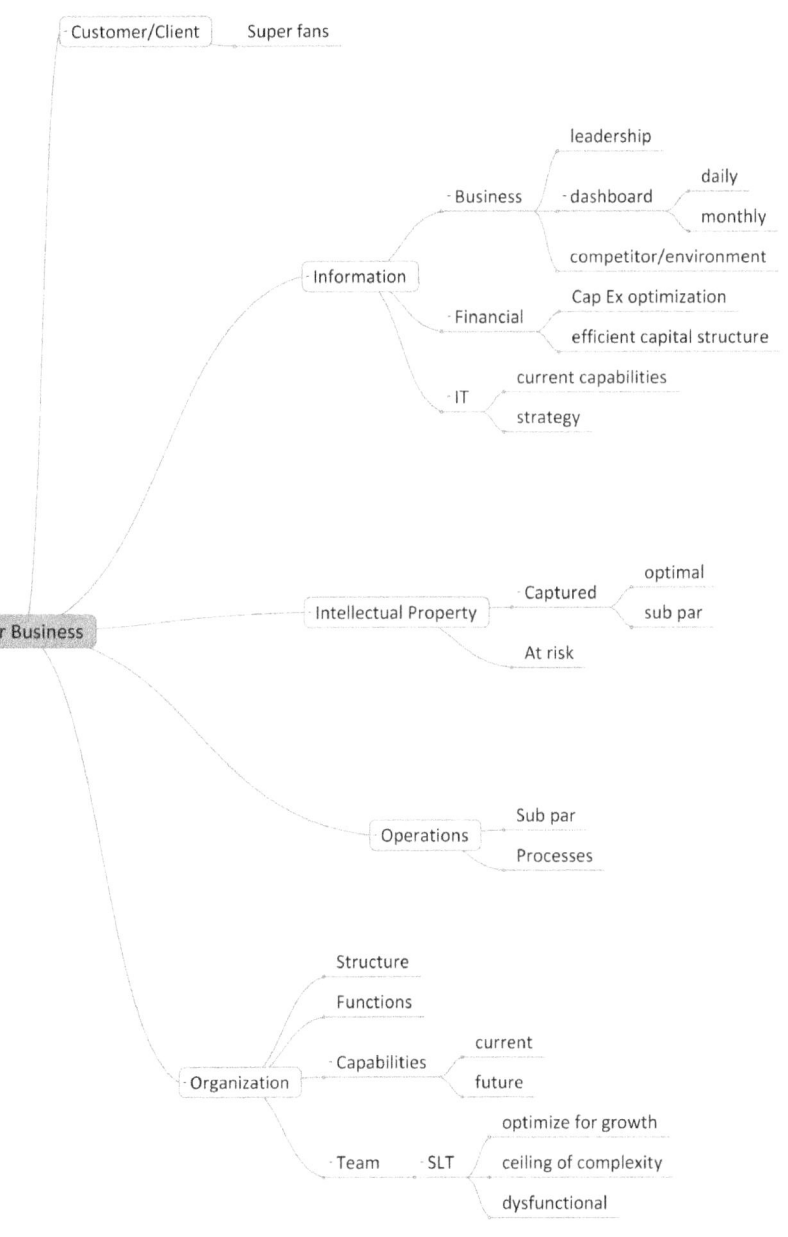

to make periodic adjustments that anticipate new market needs and choices. Adhering to the principles of business outlined in this book's chapters surely can create the necessary momentum to help your business through foggy patches. These principles will bring new business clarity and new opportunities.

In a complex world that seems bent on becoming more complex, clarity wins the day. We find people yearning to be surrounded by others who provide them clarity: if it is their barber, more visits to the barber shop; if their close business associate, more golf and lunches; if an advisor, more calls and meetings to keep and maintain clarity.

When you clearly see the path ahead, there is no holding your business back from successful execution. Business owners, like generals in battle, need a high vantage point where they can clearly see the field of battle. The field is yours to be won.

»

- **Clarity sits atop the pyramid of the other principles**
- **Mind maps support clarity**
    - » One-page graphic representation
    - » Breaks down complexities
    - » Helps to visualize connections
- **Focus on SMaC**
    - » Specific
    - » Methodical
    - » Consistent
- **Exercises in each chapter are exercises in clarity**

» SUMMING UP

Your business competes on an ever-shifting battlefield. There are challenges to face and opportunities to capitalize on.

As the leader of your company, you identify the fields, draw up the plans, establish the tactics, and support the troops.

Like any good general, you are not always leading each initiative, but you define direction and set the tone.

We have presented nine key "warrior" principles that we believe are critical to your success as a leader, and ultimately, to your company's success:

Focusing on **growth**, establishing **goals**, and developing **processes** builds the framework.

Keying on **marketing** and **innovation** and promoting **continual learning** keeps your business fresh and forward-thinking.

Leading with **confidence**, **optimism** and **clarity** inspires and spurs your team to drive onward.

Our goal for this book was to sound a bugle call for some of you, to reinforce what many of you are already practicing, and to provide some useful new tools that may come in handy in your daily battles. We hope we've stimulated your business thinking about ways you can "win the war."

» RESOURCES

Listed below are principal texts consulted during the writing of this book.

Abundance: The Future Is Better Than You Think,
      Peter H. Diamandis and Steven Kotler
      (Free Press, New York, 2012)

Drive: The Surprising Truth About What Motivates Us,
      Daniel H. Pink
      (Riverhead books, New York, 2009)

Great by Choice: Uncertainty, Chaos, and Luck–Why Some Thrive
      Despite Them All, Jim Collins and Morten T. Hansen
      (HarperCollins, New York, 2011)

The Power of Habit: Why We Do What We Do in Life and Business,
      Charles Duhigg
      (Random House, New York, 2012)

The Rational Optimist: How Prosperity Evolves,
      Matt Ridley
      (Harper Perennial, New York, 2011)

Small Giants: Companies That Choose to Be Great Instead of Big,
      Bo Burlingham
      (Penguin Group, New York, 2005)

Switch: How to Change Things When Change Is Hard,
      Chip Heath and Dan Heath
      (Broadway Books, New York, 2010)

» ACKNOWLEDGMENTS

Every book has the thumbprints of so many people on it. This one is no exception.

From artwork to research to keeping everything moving, we have been graced with an outstanding production and support team. Special thanks to Devan Adams, Jennifer Demaro, Jessica Poisl, Karyn Lachenschmidt and Kim Frank. Your energy and dedication have gotten us to the finish line.

We are grateful to our many readers who have enriched us with their own insights and helped us hone our ideas. Thank you to Sarah Komm, Tom Comiso, John Coulter, Adam Kreysar, Maribeth Kuzmeski, Stewart Flink, Steve Yastrow, Kent Pilcher, Tim Dunn, and Brian LoVetere. This book is better because of your efforts. Linn Weiss, you always know what to say and more important how to say it. Thank you.

My deepest gratitude goes to my wife, Lorena, who inspires me daily with her own entrepreneurial spirit. You live the warrior principles in your work and your life. Thank you for all the support you provide unconditionally.

While this is a joint set of acknowledgments, I want to thank Gary for showing me how 80% can create what you thought was truly impossible. Let us battle onward together.

- Adam Blonsky

» ABOUT THE AUTHORS

 **Gary Klaben** is president of Coyle Financial Counsel, a financial consulting and investment advisory services company. Over 25 years Gary has helped successful entrepreneurs, families, and corporate executives plan, execute and implement financial and wealth strategies while simplifying their complex financial lives. Through proprietary processes and systems, we deliver to clients deep support for continued growth, greater freedom and a better quality of life.

Gary's first book, *Changing the Conversation*, embodies the important non-financial issues facing his clients and their families. He has conducted dozens of seminars, workshops and webinars on various financial services subjects, and delivered conference panel talks regarding financial services. Gary graduated from West Point in 1979, with a BS in General Engineering. He served as an infantry officer in Alaska and the 82nd Airborne Division. Gary received his Chartered Financial Consultant (ChFC) designation in 1989 and Master of Science in Financial Services (MSFS) in 1995. Gary is married with two children, both graduates of West Point.

**Adam Blonsky** is an Advisor with Coyle Financial Counsel, a financial consulting and investment advisory services company. During the past 25 years, Adam has provided solutions-oriented financial counsel and corporate finance advice to families, business owners and middle market companies. His breadth of experience in the financial industry and commitment to clarity and collaboration provides each client with straight-forward, well-reasoned solutions to complex business and personal financial matters.

Adam graduated from MIT with a BS in Economics and earned his MBA from the University of Chicago Booth School of Business. Adam is married and has two children.

www.ingramcontent.com/pod-product-compliance
Lightning Source LLC
Chambersburg PA
CBHW071238170526
45165CB00003B/1152